hehehehe

G   G
ROLAND

Index

fictional dystopia scenario

every tv network shows people doing their jobs
people on drugs listen to music made to listen to
while on drugs
sincerity is hard to trust, as an option
when selling something
everything can and has been sold
it is strange to seek something still
some repeat the same 40 expressions interchangeably

hehehehe

i am now ready to accept that the customer is not right

the fascists at claire's would not pierce my penis
i have never had a wet dream
i am too good at masturbating

i need to prove to a hooker that it is just about the sex
no medical professional ever agrees to beat me up
they just laugh
sometimes the way i am makes the person i am
talking to uncomfortable, i will ask them about this
later, i will think this is all in my head
or i only associate with people who lie to me

the next time i see a dead animal on the road
i am going to kick it all the way home

russet

i want to be made into french fries
and for someone to complain about how i am not french
so i can explain that the 'french' in 'french fries'
refers to a cutting method
and that i am not a potato

im going to kill everyone until i stop getting paid

no yeah do not mind me just tying my dick in a knot
be right with you

please please please

this is a poem to a nervous people
shoegazers counting eye contact
who hate and want reciprocation and
hide from
behind their eyes

please stop, you are making others uncomfortable

communication

i want you to speak a foreign language
so i can focus on what you are saying
tell me anything
and i will smile
maybe laugh
if the noises are nice

headphones and sunglasses

it is impossible to know existence
like things are medieval
movements become debated, intentional, reflexive
after the head is
detached from the body

hehehehe

skulls always look like they are smiling

i am just waiting
for us to decompose
so my hand bones
can touch yours

the only way to line up two hearts is for one person to face away

a human heart is rubbery
and thrown against a wall
it retains its shape
unless frozen

a human heart is wet
do not hold too tightly
it will slip away

a human heart is soft
one must be gentle
maintain its integrity

a human heart is mysterious
i will never see another real one
or my own

whatever

i am korean german
a 1.5th generation american
and i steal books
but only if the authors are dead
or foreign

i hate culture that is based around something inherent
because i will never get to join in their fun
like the times i was 'white' or 'asian' to the opposite crowd

my best friend is a native american alcoholic
he can bench press over 300 pounds
once we made out while drunk and on xanax to see
if we were gay
unfortunately we are not

doodleoo

here are some things
to remember or hold dear

going crazy is not possible
if you think you are going crazy
you probably just need a nap

dreaming is a good thing
dream about small changes in your living space
a screen missing that suddenly isn't

stand outside your window
and look into your bedroom
for a better view

worry if dreams grow long
just sleep through the days
you will be okay soon

10 poems found in internet comment sections

1.
at the kennedy space center
you can touch a piece of the moon the apollo astronauts
brought back
after years and years of touching
it feels like a piece of tile

2.
whoever said she wasn't hot anymore
was blind, i want her to
ride me until the heartbreak
goes away

3.
you know
if you think a girl is sexy
half the credit is due to her father
so you gay

4.
i looked at this because almost all the plants my mom gets
die within less than a week
i think it is because she yells a lot
and sometimes i am scared of when she yells

5.
how do you deal with the fact that life sucks ass
but sometimes in the middle of the shit
a short appearance of great beauty happens, and then it
continues sucking ass

6.
we're designed to be alone
caring too much about others
who don't give a shit about us

7.
i want to be in love again
haha
i've never been in love

8.
flirtatiously
grab the roll of smarties from a girl's pocket
it's a tampon
fuck

9.
this was grim. and my worst fear
ending up lonely and middle aged
basically talking to yourself
and picking fights with service employees
but grateful
that it's live humans to talk to

10.
saying the tiger is sad because it's in the zoo
i don't think is correct
it is a pretty nice life compared to the wild
where only 1 of 8 tigers have a chance of living to an adult
here he does not go hungry
and can play and sleep
most tigers in the wild wish they could get that gig

flower poem

it is easy to write poems about flowers
they are beautiful
and die quickly
bleck

responsibility

can i touch your face
is that okay

would it be strange
if i said i hate looking at your face
the way you grew it
i feel like i am stealing

you did grow your face

on an older tv you can feel static if your face is close enough

i watch Scrubs and think "doctors are incredible"
doctors keep our hearts beating, doctors are stressed out
i watch Scrubs to learn tv doctors think life is inherently
meaningless
i eat food i do not like and think life is inherently
meaningless

doctors exist because people do not really want to die yet
i exist because i do not really want to die yet either

let me try again
let me express something close to you
so you hear, i think
i deleted this line because of fear
a tv doctor's actions have no real consequence

ifeelbad

making money just to exist, there is no happiness
no joy, no unconscious, unprepared
anything, and i worry, i text myself
for a vibration

me in a nutshell

(muffled sobbing)

some people walk around with a torture device next to their neck

i am terrified that everyone else is just a person
who also notices other people
or the bus, when it is almost here

what if every person is just like us
imagine the insanity of humans
unable to communicate

humans sometimes kill each other
and other times do the opposite
both are good or bad or something

powdered lemon flavoring

if someone believes in god
they should be in heaven, with god
communication serves a purpose
something survival related
did you know getting murdered gives you a free pass

five degrees and snowing pt. 1

you told me you are coming to where i am
i gave you vague directions and then prepared myself
for you not coming. i pulled another chair towards me
and put my feet on it. you came around
the corner and recycled something

we made eye contact and i smiled at my book
you looked at somewhere
and we looked and smiled and i felt like standing
but i took my feet off the chair
and put them on the floor

five degrees and snowing pt. 2

at age 6 you saw the hot tub sign that said '13 and up'
at age 7 you said to yourself '6 more years'
at age 8 you said to yourself '5 more years'
at age 9 you said to yourself '4 more years'
at age 10 you said to yourself '3 more years'
at age 11 you said to yourself '2 more years'
at age 12 you said to yourself '1 more year'
at age 13 you went in the hot tub
just like you did every other year
then you lived 5 more years and told me

five degrees and snowing pt. 3

there was a guy with a belly button
it looked like a third eye, or something
when he was in the room it felt weird
you felt bad about not sitting next to him

in the pool you had to share a lane
and feel like they knew you were not a swimmer

"i wish my feet would touch the ground sometimes but i like
bouncing them"
when you tell me that i feel a certain way
about not being able to express myself properly
with words

can someone pay me to say i hate money

what if an orange is not actually an orange but a banana
a study came out 40 seconds ago, this orange is a banana
'fuck' a baby yells, the mother learns
of healthy self expression and boundary testing
a serial killer named chip kills 100,000,000 people
by blowing cigarette smoke near crowds
"this is not so bad, global warming and all"
says a person wearing a t-shirt
"ha ha ha" someone says life exists in places where
humans cannot exist

fuck sincerity

would it be safe to say we are all fucks
could i assume none of us are from test tubes
one kid at my school was from a test tube

he watched porn on the bus
some people called him test tube

civil landscaping without a taxi

debate difficulty

or approach something strenuous
find a delicate direction

hard defended as useful
apt to exist as somehow needed

one needs to be up when the moon
wobbles and shines like the road

hammering glass nails into the lawn

hehehehe

the best part of drinking from the bottle is imagining
you are actually tiny, hiding in the bottom of the bottle
and can stay there forever

boiling water

i would like to wake up in a bag
a plastic bag with no windows
this is my new home

the walls are orange and sealed
there is no door
i can finally take a breath

newspapers could never find me
or question me in here
next to a seasoning packet

no one knows i am in here
that i am dry noodles now
and that is okay

hehehehe

unfortunately un-invisible prologue

i am sad
i caused this sadness myself
i love you
unless you forgot how to be soft

i want to make you laugh
but not always
i am being serious
but not always
i am trying to communicate

we are both going to die, you and me
forcing this to be precious
counted off with little movements
hilarious, heart-hurting, and stupid

i cannot say these things out loud
from a place of quiet loneliness
and self imposed isolation
this is not something to share

popsicle

1.
i have never poured lucky charms on my body
eventually they too will disappear
my favorite thing is standing on a purposefully moving
jellyfish
i have never done anything long enough
i am moving to alaska

2.
i have never met my neighbors
i move to alaska so i can never meet my neighbors
in alaska
jellyfish are exotic
other places, lucky charms

3.
jellyfish, sometimes considered in alaska
have never thrived in cold climates
i am lying about jellyfish in cold climates
i do not know about jellyfish in cold climates
i have never told the truth
i just jellyfish

4.
some jellyfish sting to pass the time
i have never squished a jellyfish under my thumbs
other jellyfish are not jellyfish because they are turtles
tomorrow alaska says all new residents bring jellyfish
i want to experience death because of jellyfish

5.
hi alaska
i am at home on my street
stand with me on the sidewalk
there is a jellyfish parade today
would you like some lucky charms?

some have trouble biting ice or drinking cold water because of the painful sensation

every morning i lie in the street
and put earplugs in
so when i chew ice cubes they are loud

some days my mouth shivers
and when the ice cubes melt
a little water spills out of my mouth

viagra is for pussies

tomorrow my penis gets upgraded
for better sex, increased confidence, detachment
i underhand toss my upgraded penis
it softly thumps against her forehead
she says "wow, is that upgraded?"
i say "it is detachable"
she tells me she wants to throw it
i am sorry about the title
please give me my penis back

self improvement

i am trying to soften my eyes
so things can sink into them
slowly, deliberately
like pine needles in jellyfish

hehehehe

i like to masturbate with headphones on and the door unlocked in case a robber comes

i cum on a robber
i am a hero
imagine the headlines
i am congratulated for cumming
finally

santa cruz, ca

i am digging when you show up
if i dig enough i will not reach china
i will reach some part of the ocean
you sit on the edge of the hole
you swing your feet and smile at me
i like the way you look there
i sit next to you and the wall crumbles
you say we are a little closer to china

hurricane jasmine

water hair brown by nature
and every freckle, you

i will drown behind your ear
then float forever, sometimes
brushing against your neck

socks

i bought a space heater
for everywhere i go, like outside
i plug in, keep my feet warm

you walk onto a pond in the middle of winter
make noises again like laughing then
sit in the space the sun makes
between two clouds, when the snow stops
i sit down inside and eat a grapefruit
peel and all

i know

1.
you will not absolutely hate this poem
you will not tell me that you absolutely hate this poem in the
form of a short film
you will not show me you wrote a novel, a medium play
then burn the only copies

2.
it will not snow
if it snows or does not snow i am going to confront it
i am going to wrestle it into submission then wrap it in
newspaper and sell it by the pound

3.
something non-human can do human things in stories and
poems
a reader can identify with something non-human in a story
or poem
an animal can do things that are figurative but sensical

4.
every word i have ever seen has been a guess
and from what i understand, i am illiterate
i do not know
i love you

boat poem

our boat–a dream
canoe: for two

giggle, hm, beam
a more?
(i see–three?)

and so, to shore
to fit, one more
just for, this chore
no more, we four

sink

why the long face

i was sleeping
someone replaced my head
with a plank of wood

i do not know what they wanted
but i cannot fit through doors anymore

canned fruit

we could go to the grocery store together
and people will ask if he is steve buscemi and
he will say yes i am with his steve buscemi voice
and look back at them with his steve buscemi eyes
steve buscemi is my best friend

steve buscemi kisses a baby on the head
with lips he grew in a laboratory
these are top of the line
he assures me

steve buscemi is unsure if he can go on in hollywood
i sense his indecision
and that creates worry

steve buscemi is an alien with laboratory lips
steve buscemi is my best friend

tomorrow steve buscemi quits acting and goes back to
space
but today we are grocery shopping

i had to steal the bike pump because the clerk told me it was only for inflating tires

my ears flap hard against the walls
a balsa wood cube contains a balloon
the house leaves small indentations that fade

tether-less, my face crushes a town
inhabitants take pictures but it doesn't matter
i bury them with the dark skin under my eyes

the clouds are just water
aliens fly by and keep their heads down
the entire universe, my face

steam

i spin my wheels of hate to the hate station
fill the car with hate, get a nice hot cup of hate
full of hate, i drive hate miles over the hate limit
the hate police say "i hate you"
i say "i hate you too"
they let me off with a warning

pressure change

a baby is crying on an airplane
"get a fuckin load of this guy" i say to other passengers
i point at the baby with my fists, it has a little hat on
"that is a baby. it does not know it is a baby" someone says
i rip the side of my five pound paper bag of sugar and
shake it empty
the baby looks at me
i tip the hat off the baby's head "hey fuck you man"
the baby licks its arm and rolls its head back
i point to a poem "do you understand this"
i jam my poetry book into the baby's face and it cries
"you do not even know the sham-wow is a sham" i say
quietly
the baby licks the corner of its chin
i call for the stewardess, then stand on my seat
i take off my shoes and wave them in the baby's face
the stewardess asks me to sit down
"this baby can not even tie my shoes"
i feel a hot tear
the baby looks me in the eye and shits itself
i collapse in my seat, sobbing
"now is that better?" says the stewardess
sugar is everywhere

seoul

uncles give me money and touch my hair and cheek
"james dean, james dean" says my aunt
she claps and smiles
my brother and i ride the subway
my dad knocks over a pile of rocks at a buddhist temple
i say 'the point of those rocks isn't the point'
"i am the tallest one on the subway" says my brother
"i am the tallest one on the escalator" says my dad
in america, everyone eats wheat and children leave at 18
in korea, rice and seafood are the norm
at home a single 30 year old schoolteacher
uses a plastic u-shaped massager on her face
to make it smaller
because that is attractive in korea

yo

i wear sunglasses or headphones
maybe both
i do not want to be where i am
i wear headphones and take one out
to make sure i'm still breathing
or maybe i am breathing too much and should stop
having music in both ears makes me feel barely insane
behind sunglasses, my eyes could be anything
i challenge people i see walking around, sometimes get
right in their way
"you do not know where i am looking"
then i tap on my sunglasses with my thumbnails

"please, i am going to be late" they sometimes reply
i smile and do a cartwheel with bent legs

standing at a crosswalk

i want to cover my face
like a mold for papier mâché
but i will use duct tape instead

you look at me and i will not know
behind dull grey 2 inch wide strips

after a week i will want light on my face
and the sun in my eyes
i think

i will take off the mask
starting at my hairline
and rip it down
deliberately
with glee

my cheeks raise and the edges of my mouth
indicate a smile
it is coming off
i can not close my eyes
i am just red

old animal interacting with a small animal

1.
some people will not die
i communicate to them about feeling hopeless haha
they say yeah it is okay eventually
everyday i wake up at 5 am and can not stop coughing
i think of all the saddest things on a shelf
all of them in neat lines
people dying every second
i will never see them
i curl in a ball, unable to compensate
for how un-sad they are
the news runs a new series
i am sad

2.
one christmas my brother and i were taken to a puppy farm
a beagle named snoopy ran in the street
before six months liquid filled his lungs and he was
in a white cardboard box with a rose taped to the front
snoopy got buried on a hill and i cried but i did not
love that dog
i did not know him. when we were at home my mom picked
out burrs
my brother and i appreciated what she did for our socks
and shoes
somehow i became the greatest fear in my own life

1 in 3,500,000,000

looking for a girl who does not take things too seriously
a woman skilled at making jokes at her own expense
unable to say anything positive about herself

she has low self esteem
is incapable of joy
lacks the energy for suicide

gosh it would be swell
meeting such a lady

planning

my coffin is in 12 parts and fits in a gun
the gun is dropped into a regular coffin
only that coffin is shaped like a bullet
and my grave hole looks like a gun

a service is held in silence
the pastor cowboyspins a revolver, holsters it
and hands out ammunition

at my wake it is raining
everyone stands outside
shooting clouds they dislike
no one dares sing over the gunfire

art history

1.

michelangelo sometimes felt self conscious while carving
or drawing dicks
he would pretend to be working on another part of the art if
he heard someone coming
often he was not fast enough or too focused
a pope would say "mike,
you have been working on that dick for at least 8 days
what do you say we move on? maybe the shoulders
could use some work?"

2.

in the bottom
right corner
of that ceiling
of the sistine mural
is a drawing
of a dick
covered
by that pope's face

3.

the medici family is discussed in the town square
"they are financing artists to paint and sculpt dicks!"

4.
in a social situation michelangelo says "sorry
but i need to get back to the vatican
i gotta finish shading
jesus's dick"

5.
michelangelo and da vinci engage
in painting competitions
but just
measure dicks

if being punk is not caring then i will care too much because i do not care about not caring about being punk

with this new knife i make a big cut
then squish my brain into a display box
and say "well isn't that nice" and you agree

you say "you should have died by now"
i say "probably, but
brain surgery is unique
the brain does not need anesthetics"
you laugh and prod the box

if i were an armadillo i would probably die of dehydration

the plant you gave me is dying
i wish i had intentionally not watered it
because it would feel good
to do that and feel good about it

sometimes i wish you and everyone else were assholes
so i could say 'fuck you' and feel good doing so
but i can not, so i will not

is it normal to want to hate everyone you meet
preemptively, so you can feel powerful and bizarre
like you're wearing a big sieve used for draining noodles
like you're an armadillo, ready to roll up at any time

criss angel's last performance

an elephant disappears in a parking lot
he says it is missing
i do not know where it is. please help me
this keeps happening. the elephant was just here. now it is
gone.
i do not know. maybe not. we will die eventually.
"stop not doing magic" says the crowd to criss angel
"i am a buddhist" says criss angel back

all that is right and all that is left

i am going to chop off my left arm
and you are going to chop off your right arm
so we can lie facing each other
comfortably

dick-b

one of the algorithms helps me meet you
another helps me find more grape flavored candy

so instead of putting my ashes (when i die)
into the great big ash pile

find a way to get us into an algorithm
so two other humans can love

hehehehe

let's talk about your tattoos

sometimes i feel like a serial killer or something
with how obsessed i can get with who you are
i promise i will not kill you

all i am going to do is put my mouth on every part of your
skin

hunter/hunted

though i will never kill
i will shoot you

i will capture you
maybe me too

and we will be forever
unmoving, close
together

poem to the shape of a person

stop following me
i want to be alone
it has to be dark

walking music

sing another song with me
with only fingers
we play at each other, our eyes closed
pressing, pausing only to smile

american dream

i release an album of 23 tracks that average 2.5 minutes
ranging from 13 seconds (an intro song)
to 9 minutes (a ballad)
the 58 minute album will be 58 minutes of silence
critics rave "a sonic masterpiece"
i win every award, especially military ones
new music blog websites are created
thissongissilent.com gets 400 downloads a minute
for a month
the deaf community meets with speaker conglomerates
a team of opera tenor hitmen stalk me and i hire bodyguards
so i can sleep

fluttering not pinned and mounted

i could not share this meal with anyone else
who but you would want to sit, to settle
to grow caterpillars in the belly

quality

sometimes people go to the store
and think
"this is the last toothbrush i will ever buy"

About G. G. Roland

GG Roland lives in Colorado. He enjoys shovelling snow.

ALSO BY CLASH BOOKS

LIFE OF THE PARTY
Tea Hacic-Vlahovic

THE ELVIS MACHINE
Kim Vodicka

TRY NOT TO THINK BAD THOUGHTS
Matthew Revert

FOGHORN LEGHORN
Big Bruiser Dope Boy

99 POEMS TO CURE WHATEVER'S WRONG WITH YOU OR CREATE THE PROBLEMS YOU NEED
Sam Pink

50 BARN POEMS
Zac Smith

NAKED
Joel Amat Güell

HORROR FILM POEMS
Christoph Paul

TRASH PANDA
Leza Cantoral

REGRET OR SOMETHING MORE ANIMAL
Heather Bell

ALL THE PLACES I WISH I DIED
Crystal Stone

WE PUT THE LIT IN LITERARY
clashbooks.com

@clashbooks   @clashbooks   /clashbooks

Email
clashmediabooks@gmail.com

Publicity
McKenna Rose
clashbookspublicity@gmail.com